Healthcare Sector

Erik Johnson
Copyright © 2020 FYMM

All rights reserved.

ISBN:

9798587255579

HealthCare

CONTENTS

1	Pfizer	1
2	UnitedHealth Group	5
3	Johnson & Johnson	8
4	Sarepta Therapeutics	15
5	Bristol-Myers Squibb	18
6	Moderna	22
7	Merck	26
8	AstraZeneca	29
9	Abbvie	33
10	Gilead Sciences	37

1 PFIZER

Pfizer is the next company we will discuss over the last 5 years this company has been pretty stagnant it consistently pays dividends but the growth has been non-existent. On their website they have a cool tool that you can use to show where your investment would be if you invested in Pfizer or one of the major indexes. Since January 2019 you with a $10,000 investment you would be down $2,000 investment Pfizer but you would be up for thousand dollars investing in the S&P 500.

A few well-known products for Pfizer are Lipitor Zoloft and Viagra. Pfizer is a genius when it comes to their products because Zoloft is an antidepressant with a side effect of erectile dysfunction now if you have erectile dysfunction then the product you were going to buy is another Pfizer product in Viagra.

The company manages its operations through two segments Pfizer Innovative health and Pfizer Essential Health.

Pfizer was also the first company to get United States emergency approval for a coronavirus vaccine.

2 UNITEDHEALTH GROUP

UnitedHealth Group stock ticker UNH. Over the past five years this company has traditionally gone higher with it closed with all-time highs. Coronavirus did not do too much damage to this company in the long run; it actually has helped this company. UnitedHealth Group provides a plethora of products Hospital Solutions and also insurance for its recipients.

They do not pay very much in a dividend at only one and a half percent but they've consistently paid that dividend over a course of many years.

The company operates in four different segments United Healthcare Optum health optuminsight and Optum RX. The institutional ownership of this company is in line with what I like to see above 80%. With an actual number being 89% institutional ownership

3 JOHNSON & JOHNSON

Johnson & Johnson can be broken up into three different departments; consumer Health Products, medical devices, in pharmaceutical products.

Consumer Health Products :

Their products are in almost every convenient or grocery store across the United States their brands help people live healthier lives through skin Health Products, self c
are products, and Essential Health Products,

Skin Health Products :

A few of thier skin Health products are Neutrogena which has been bringing customers Skin Care Solutions for more than sixty years in available in more than 70 countries, Aveeno which is available in 22 countries worldwide, DR.CI:LABO Was founded by renowned Japanese dermatologist Dr. Yoshinori Shirono in 1999.

Self care products:

if you've ever needed to use Tylenol Motrin Zyrtec or Benadryl even Nicorette you are using a Johnson & Johnson product. those are just a few to name in Johnson Johnson's arsenal of self care products.

Essential Health Products:

For 125 years Johnson & Johnson has provided gentle products for babies and adults if you've ever needed a Band-Aid a recognizable brand Band-Aid is also a Johnson & Johnson product. a mouthwash that has been used over a billion times and is in 85 different countries is also a Johnson & Johnson product by the name of Listerine.

Medical devices:

and then always changing environment Johnson & Johnson are making the correct connections across Science and Technology to combine their expertise in Vision, Orthopedics, Interventional Solutions and surgery.

Pharmaceutical products

 in Johnson & Johnson's labs the address some of the most devastating and complex diseases known to man. Their

pharmaceutical company is Janssen pharmaceutical companies their main purpose is changing the way diseases are prevented intercepted treated and cured diseases that they focus on are; Immunology, Cardiovascular & Metabolic Disease, Pulmonary Hypertension
Infectious Diseases & Vaccines, Neuroscience, Oncology

4 SAREPTA THERAPEUTICS

Sarepta Therapeutics stock ticker srpt. This company is at all-time high over the last 5 years you can see it's out of trouble breaking out of the 150 level but since is that 175 during the corona they dipped slightly but reached an all-time high before July then dipped and in December sarepta is once again at an all-time high.

This company would be classified more as a growth stock since it does not pay dividends. Sarepta Therapeutics is a biopharmaceutical company that focuses on Discovery and development of ribose nucleic acid (RNA)-targeted therapeutics which is the treatment of rare neuromuscular diseases.

The company is located in Cambridge Massachusetts The institutional ownership of this company is quite high at 92%

5 BRISTOL-MYERS SQUIBB

Bristol-Myers Squibb:

Their main focus is research and therapeutic areas where they believe they can deliver transformational medicines to patients. right now they are studying more than 40 different diseases and they have over 50 compounds in development.

Translational medicine

This is a rapidly growing discipline in the biomedical research its purpose is to expedite the discovery of new diagnostic tools and treatments. With their world class researchers and their long history of translating scientific learning Bristol-Myers Squibb strives to uncover life-changing treatments for the most challenging diseases of now and the future.

Through their research and development division they're looking to develop drugs for solid tumors, lung problems, head and neck issues, Esophageal, Gastroesophageal, Glioblastoma, To name a few.

A notable one of its subsidiaries is Celgene Corp. Celgene is a pharmaceutical company that makes cancer and Immunology drugs Their major product in their pipeline is Revlimid

6 MODERNA

moderna stock ticker mRNA. If we analyzed their stock price over the last 10 years or 5 years you will see that they've been under a $30 company until the beginning of this year. What is very interesting about this company is since Inception which was 2018 this company has lost 1.5 billion dollars and they lost 500 million alone in 2019. In early 2020 the CEO of moderna told the president that they would be able to have a vaccine for Coronavirus and since then their stock has went from under $25 to over $130. The company was awarded over four hundred million dollars from operation of warp speed to bring a solution or vaccine to the market. This company does not pay a dividend. Institutional ownership for this stock is quite low at 52%. What concerns me the most about this company is days before the government approved their coronavirus vaccine it is seen in their sec filings, Many of the top directors of the company sold their stock, the CEO of the company in one transaction turned $400,000 into 13 million dollars. It raises the question if you believed in your company and the products why would you cash out at the beginning of the ride. to me the only reason someone would Cash Out millions of dollars is they are not a firm believer in their product or their company and it sounds like a traditional pump and dump.

7 MERCK

Merck stock Ticker MRK. Over the last five years the stock price has consistently gone higher. It looks as if the all-time high was at the beginning of 2020. Since coronavirus happened it has regained most of the coronavirus drop but it has yet to break out of all-time highs. The institutional ownership is at 75% which is a little lower than I like to see which is at 80%.

The company operates in four segments pharmaceutical Animal Health healthcare services and alliances. Their vaccine products consists of prevented pediatric, Adolescent and adult vaccines.

Merck pays 3.3% dividend annually.

8 ASTRAZENECA

Astrazeneca:

They have 172 projects in their pipeline, 9 new molecular entries in their late stage pipeline and one new molecular entry to registration, The therapy areas AstraZeneca is focused on are oncology, Cardiovascular, Renal & Metabolism, Respiratory and Immunology. They're also discovering different solutions to more of life's problems such as diabetic neuropathy, Parkinson's disease, Alzheimer's disease, opiate use disorder and the prevention of nosocomial Staphylococcus aureus pneumonia.

They have three major locations with one in Gaithersburg Maryland this campus employees more than 3,000 experts. Their second location is in Gothenburg Sweden with more than 2,400 employees from 50 different countries. and their main location located in Cambridge United Kingdom. boasting that Cambridge is one of the most exciting bioscience locations in the world providing over 19,000 local jobs and more than 440 life science and health care organizations.

9 ABBVIE

Abbvie:

Is a biopharmaceutical company founded in 2013. Its original company was Abbott Laboratories but they decided to break Abbott

Laboratories into two different publicly traded companies so investors would be able to Value the company separately with Abbott Laboratories specializing in Diversified products including medical devices, diagnostic equipment and nutrition products and AbbVie would operate as a research-based pharmaceutical manufacturer.

Their Ventures team is comprised of seven investment professionals across three major Us locations

Cambridge Massachusetts Chicago Illinois and San Francisco California.

The company's main focus areas are Immunology oncology neuroscience Women's Health platforms and Technology, Cystic fibrosis And Virology.

One of their largest and most profitable Acquisitions to date happened May 8th 2020 when they completed the acquisition of Allergan. By buying Allergan they have bought a well-seasoned pipeline of different products already available on the market such as Botox.

10 GILEAD SCIENCES

Gilead Sciences

we look over five years they were really popular in 2015 but as of right now they're kind of going down institutional ownership 80% I do like that, They are making a lot of money from Remdesivir, this drug was approved as an emergency treatment in hospitals. They originally created this drug to help fight against ebola. Since this is a repurpose drug the costs associated with production are very low. They recommended a 5 day treatment with a value of 2300$ The cost to the company per five day treatment is 5$. These numbers are rounded to the nearest whole number, however as we see they are making close to 2295$ per Covid19 hospital treatment. Remdesivir is approved in australia, canada, the european union japan and the United States.

The company is at a seven year low, however they have consistently been able to pay about 4% annual dividend.

In other news they signed an agreement to provide 200K prescriptions of their HIV drug for 11 years for free to the recipient but the government will reimburse them 200$ per 30 pills .

www.ingramcontent.com/pod-product-compliance
Lightning Source LLC
Chambersburg PA
CBHW072237230526
45466CB00024B/2087